Sir Francis Drake

Discover The Life Of An Explorer

Trish Kline

Rourke
Publishing LLC
Vero Beach, Florida 32964

www.rourkepublishing.com

PHOTO CREDITS: IRC-www.historypictures.com: cover, title page; pages 8, 10, 13, 14, 15, 21; © Hulton/Archive by Getty Images: pages 4, 7, 17, 18.

Title page: Sir Francis Drake was greeted as a king by Indians in California.

Editor: Frank Sloan

Cover design by Nicola Stratford

Library of Congress Cataloging-in-Publication Data

Kline, Trish.
   Sir Francis Drake / Trish Kline
      p. cm. — (Discover the life of an explorer)
   Summary: A biography of the English seaman and explorer who became the first man from England to sail around the world.
   Includes bibliographical references and index.
   ISBN 1-58952-295-8
   1. Drake, Francis, Sir, 1540? - 1596—Juvenile literature. 2. Great Britain—History, Naval—Tudors, 1485-1603—Biography—Juvenile literature.
3. Great Britain—History—Elizabeth, 1558-1603—Biography—Juvenile literature. 4. Explorers—Great Britain—Biography—Juvenile literature.
5. Admirals—Great Britain—Biography—Juvenile literature. [1. Drake, Francis, Sir, 1540? - 1596. 2. Explorers. 3. Admirals.] I. Title.

DA86.22.D7 K58 2002
942.05'5'092—dc21   2002017048

Printed in the USA

CG/CG

TABLE OF CONTENTS

DREAMS

Francis Drake was born in England, around 1541. His family was poor. They lived in an old ship. This began Drake's love of the sea.

Drake first went to sea when he was 12. He worked on a small ship. He wanted to learn to be a captain. When the owner of the ship died, he gave the boat to Drake. Drake sold the ship. But he did not give up his dream of being a captain.

Francis Drake spent most of his life sailing the world's oceans.

A GREAT PIRATE

In 1567, a relative asked Drake to sail with him. He made Drake captain of one of his ships. Together, they made three **voyages**. They bought slaves. They took these slaves to the New World.

In 1572, Drake led his ships in attacks on Spanish seaports. He robbed the Spanish ships of their cargo. He returned to England with his ship full of Spanish silver. Drake became known as a great pirate.

A ship belonging to Francis Drake

DRAKE ATTACKS

In 1577, Queen Elizabeth I of England was **jealous** of the great **empire** Spain had in the New World. She asked Drake to attack Spanish **settlements**.

Drake's ships sailed to South America. He attacked the Spanish settlements in the present-day countries of Chile and Peru. He also attacked Spanish ships carrying silver. Drake took the **treasure** for himself and for the queen of England.

Queen Elizabeth I sent Drake to attack Spanish settlements in the New World.

AROUND THE WORLD

Drake then sailed to North America. He stopped for repairs near present-day San Francisco. He claimed the land known today as California for the queen of England.

Drake met Indians in California when he stopped to repair his ship.

Drake sailed south across the Pacific and Indian oceans. He then went around the southern tip of Africa. The voyage was very long. It took three years. But this voyage was important to England. It made him the first person from England to sail around the world.

Drake's ships sailed into South American ports.

Drake traded for spices and supplies during his travels.

Drake claimed land for England near present-day San Francisco.
He named the land New Albion.

A HERO RETURNS

In the winter of 1580, Drake returned to England. The queen was very happy with the treasure. She said that Drake was a hero. She said that, from that time forward, Francis Drake would be called *Sir* Francis Drake.

Drake is knighted by Queen Elizabeth I.

BURIED AT SEA

In 1585, England **declared** war with Spain. Sir Francis Drake again went to sea. His ships destroyed many great Spanish warships.

In 1596, while at sea, Drake became ill. Soon, he died. His body was placed inside a lead **casket.** The casket was dropped into the sea. Two ships were sunk near his body. He was about 55 years old.

Drake died from an illness and was buried at sea.

ENGLAND'S GREAT NAVIGATOR

Sir Francis Drake was the first English **navigator** to travel around the world. His voyage increased the knowledge of the **geography** of the world. His discovery of present-day California led to English settlements in North America.

Drake was one of the best known English explorers.

IMPORTANT DATES TO REMEMBER

1541?   Born in England

1553   First went to sea

1567   Voyage to bring slaves to the New World

1572   Attacked and robbed Spanish ships

1577   Attacked Spanish settlements in the
          New World

1580   First English person to sail around the world

1596   Died at about age 55

GLOSSARY

casket (KAS kit) — box or coffin in which the dead are buried

declare (dee KLAYR) — to speak or make known

empire (EM pyre) — a large kingdom or nation

geography (jee AHG re fee) — the study of the Earth and its plants and animals

jealous (JEL es) — wanting what another has or owns

navigator (NAV i gayt er) — one who guides or pilots, such as captain of a ship

settlements (SET uhl mentz) — small villages or towns

treasure (TREZH er) — a very large amount of riches, such as jewels and gold

voyages (VOY ij ez) — trips to faraway places

INDEX

Further Reading

Gallagher, Jim. *Sir Francis Drake and the Foundation of a World Empire*. Chelsea House Publishing, 2000.

Gerrard, Ray. *Sir Francis Drake: His Daring Deeds*. Sunburst, 1999.

Websites To Visit

www.mariner.org (The Mariner's Museum, Newport News, VA)

www.nmm.ac.uk (The National Maritime Museum, London, England)

www.smithsonianmag.com (*Smithsonian* magazine)

About The Author

Trish Kline has written a great number of nonfiction books for the school and library market. Her publishing credits include two dozen books, as well as hundreds of newspaper and magazine articles, anthologies, short stories, poetry, and plays. She lives in Helena, Montana.